Healing From Sexual Abuse

An Adlerian Play Therapy Approach

A workbook by

Brighter Tomorrows Consulting

Printed by CreateSpace
Self-Published by Brighter Tomorrows Consulting, LLC
1815 North Expressway, Suite B
Griffin, Georgia 30223
www.brighter-tomorrows.com

Acknowledgments:

BTC Staff Publication Credit (Work for Hire)

Shannon M. Eller, LPC, LMFT, CPCS,

AAMFT-Approved Supervisor

Candace Reagin, BS

Annthony Duffey, MSW

Contents

ix

Introduction

This workbook represents an Adlerian Play Therapist's approach to counseling and supporting sexually abused clients. It is organized into four therapeutic stages, which are denoted at the top-left corner of each activity:

- **Bridging & Rapport Building,**
- **Identifying Presenting Problem(s),**
- **Treatment, and**
- **Recovery & Maintenance.**

Each of these therapeutic stages consists of several workbook activities that work together to convey which thoughts, feelings, and experiences should be dealt with as well as which skills should be learned at each stage. Undertaken in sequence, the sections will guide you and your client through the healing process unto normalization of healthy, functional sexual practices.

A wealth of evidence-based research in social science supports the aptitude, value, and success of play therapy as a clinical approach—especially to victims of trauma and abuse. Play therapy attempts to facilitate a therapeutic space and relationship wherein clients are permitted and encouraged to become self-directing in a socially responsible way. There are multiple theoretical approaches to play therapy; this workbook adopts that of Alfred Adler, the theorist behind Individual Psychology. Adlerian Play Therapy maintains/theorizes that subjects are not pathological, but are disconnected, discounted, discouraged, or disempowered. Thus, symptomology or problem behavior is borne of some interruption or corruption of successful attainment of what Adler calls Crucial C's: **Connect, Count, Courage, and Capable.**

Children need to feel connected to individuals in their lives, ranging from family to friends to role models. They also need to feel that they count, that they matter, and that they are important to the people with whom they are connected, specifically, and to the world, generally. Children need to feel encouraged so that they may make decisions for themselves and face responsibility for those decisions. Last, children need to feel empowered and, thus, capable of responsible self-direction.

This workbook maintains an explicit focus on 'Capable' as is appropriate for victims of abuse. Sexual abuse can cause feelings of isolation for fear of disclosure, guilt, or shame. It can also create a sense in its victims that they do not matter or that they are as worthless as the objects they are sometimes treated as. Victims of sexual abuse are discouraged and often fail to report abuse for fear of unknown consequences. Lastly, victims are disempowered by their perpetrators to the point that they often imagine themselves unable to stop the abuse they suffer. Sexual abuse negatively and significantly affects each of Adler's Crucial C's. Each of the activities in this workbook will speak to at least one of Adler's Crucial C's. The Crucial C that an activity addresses is listed in the upper-right corner of each activity.

Drawing upon major veins in the Play Therapists' repertoire, this workbook offers easy and engaging play therapy interventions for each activity. These Play Prescriptions are of three major types:

- **Expressive Arts Therapy—visual arts,**
- **Music & Kinesthetic Therapies—music, dance, kinetic, and**
- **Narrative Therapy—storytelling and puppetry arts.**

While the activities provide the group with a guided education element to the psychoeducational project in this workbook, these Play Prescriptions offer an independent study element which will promote reflection, introspection, and reinforcement of lessons. Depending on the age of your client, he or she will engage differently with each Play Prescription. While younger clients may be content to doodle, clang-and-clack, or put on puppet shows, older clients may engage in fine arts, musical composition, or creative writing.

Each activity will link to at least one type of Play Prescription as is marked in the lower-left corner of each activity. Some Play Prescriptions may encompass more than one type of therapy. While play-therapeutic supplies can be acquired on an ad hoc basis as a client works through this workbook, it will best accompany an already existing, furnished, and stocked play therapy room. This will allow for creativity as a client sees fit, for more than the suggested tools and supplies will be at hand.

As with any therapeutic approach, there are a few caveats that warrant attention. This workbook is primarily oriented toward the perspective, cognitive capacities, and interests of children. If you are implementing this workbook in therapy with an adult survivor of sexual abuse, some of the activities or interventions may not be appropriate. Feel free and encouraged to adapt them to your population(s) or skip over some of them in order to ensure age-appropriateness and to safeguard intervention efficacy. For insight on adaptation, see the bibliography in the back of this workbook for references to the theories that underlie the interventions. This should ensure an appropriate and clinically sound approach to any adaptations you find necessary or useful. Lastly, always be mindful of the possibility of suicidality in clients. Confronting trauma can often precipitate extreme emotional reactions and suicidality can be among these. See the section, later in this workbook, regarding assessment of suicidality in the play therapy setting as well as the bibliography for reference to other materials on suicidality.

Your clients will play their way to adjustment, empowerment, and capability. Let this workbook guide your approach to working with victims of sexual abuse and complement your own clinical insight to re-fit the hands of the abused with the tools of self-direction!

Key & Legend

KEY

Activity Number

Activity Title

Adlerian Crucial C

Therapeutic Stage

A C T I V I T Y

Play Prescription Type Icon

I.6   Ouch! Trauma Hurts   CAPABLE, COURAGE

Like you learned in the last activity, a trauma can change us and make it difficult to get back to the way we were before. A trauma can make us nervous, interrupt our thoughts, or make our bodies do things that we feel like we can't control. It can also make us feel sad, angry, or scared for a long time. It is hard to feel the way we did before, especially when our thoughts seem so out of control. Sometimes, we can even feel like we are crazy... but that's not true! The way you have been feeling since your trauma is normal. That is what is supposed to happen to us after a trauma.

Complete a picture of yourself below that shows how you have been feeling since your trauma happened.

Normalizing Traumatic Response   15

Play Prescription Name

Workbook Page Number

LEGEND

Expressive Arts Therapy   Kinesthetic & Music Therapy   Narrative Therapy

Therapeutic Stage I — Bridging & Rapport-Building

1

In this therapeutic stage, it is unrealistic to expect a client to be able early on to delve deeply into sensitive, painful issues such as sexual trauma. This particular stage is designed to facilitate rapport building as well as establishment of the therapeutic relationship and a sense of trust and safety with the clinician. Bridging is a therapeutic modality designed to lessen the space between the client and the clinician, the unconscious, subconscious, and conscious memory, and the client's past, present, and future experiences. The activities and interventions in this section may, but may not necessarily, create an entryway to the client trauma. Rapport building is the establishment of a safe, private, and non-judgmental environment in which the client has the permission to self-express their deepest unspoken secrets and experiences related to their trauma. In this stage, the clinician strives to establish an egalitarian relationship with the client.

The use of Rogerian Common Factors is essential to both the bridging process and rapport building. Common Factors can be understood to include:

- **Genuineness / Congruency,**
- **Unconditional Positive Regard,**
- **Warmth,**
- **Trust,**
- **Immediacy,**
- **Respect,**
- **Empathy, and**
- **Acceptance**

The clinician's employment of these factors, alongside a strong sense of self, will allow the client the space, freedom, and safety needed to address trauma in therapeutic session. Though this is the shortest therapeutic stage, it is the stage upon which the success of all the others follows. Take time and care in this brief but crucial therapeutic stage.

Draw a picture of yourself doing something in the box below. Add as much detail as you want. Then fill in the blanks on the next page so we can get to know each other better!

My name is _____

and I am _____ years old. I live in _____

with _____.

I go to a school called _____ where I really like to

_____.

I really like _____,

and I enjoy _____.

I don't like _____,

and I don't enjoy _____.

When I grow up, I want to _____

_____.

One thing I'm really good at is _____.

and one thing my friends like about me is _____.

I think I'm here because _____

_____.

What I have been told about why I am here is _____

_____.

I feel _____ about being here and I feel

_____about the person I am here to see.

4

Think about your family for a moment. How many people in your family have helped you before? It could be something as simple as helping you with your chores and homework, or as important as helping you make a big decision. You'll probably discover that every single person in your family has helped you in some way before. You've probably also helped all of them in return. These people aren't just your family members. They are your helpers!

Make a list of your family members below. For each person in your family, write one way that they help you and one way that you help them.

_____ is a member of my family.

This person has helped me by _____.

I have helped this person by _____.

_____ is a member of my family.

This person has helped me by _____.

I have helped this person by _____.

_____ is a member of my family.

This person has helped me by _____.

I have helped this person by _____.

_____ is a member of my family.

This person has helped me by _____.

I have helped this person by _____.

_____ is a member of my family.

This person has helped me by _____.

I have helped this person by _____.

If you run out of room for your family, just add another sheet! Fit them all in!

 Kinetic Family Drawing

Did you know that you have helpers outside your family? Just like you thought of how your family members help you and you help them, you probably have people like that at school, at church, or other places. If you think really hard you'll probably be able to come up with a list of other helpers that's *even bigger* than the list you made of your family helpers. Don't forget your teachers, doctors, and people at church.

Make a list of your other helpers below. For each helper outside your family, write how you know them and write one way that they help you.   Don't forget new helpers!

_____ is a helper; I know them from _____.

This person has helped me by _____.

_____ is a helper; I know them from _____.

This person has helped me by _____.

_____ is a helper; I know them from _____.

This person has helped me by _____.

_____ is a helper; I know them from _____.

This person has helped me by _____.

_____ is a helper; I know them from _____.

This person has helped me by _____.

_____ is a helper; I know them from _____.

This person has helped me by _____.

_____ is a helper; I know them from _____.

This person has helped me by _____.

If you run out of room for your other helpers, just add another sheet! Fit them all in!

Kinetic Community Drawing

You have probably heard a few new words come into your life recently. Now that your helpers know what happened, they need a way to talk with other helpers about it. This makes it easier for them to get you the exact help you need as quickly as possible.

One of the new words you might recognize is "**TRAUMA**." Do you know what this word means? A trauma is something that happens to us that is so scary that it changes us in some way and makes it difficult to get back to the way we were before. It is an event that our thoughts, feelings, and bodies are not prepared to handle. A trauma can be something startling like being in a car accident, something sad like losing someone we love, or something scary like being chased by an angry dog. It all depends on the person it happens to.

What do we mean when we say that it can be difficult to get back to the way we were before? Before your trauma, you were a certain way. In short, life was probably a little bit better before your trauma. What we have to do when we have a trauma is to try to get back to the way we were before. There is a lot of work that goes into it, but that's what we have to try to do. That's what you're doing right this moment!

Circle the items below that YOU think are examples of trauma.

Somebody makes you drop
your ice cream cone.

Your parents scream at each
other when they are angry.

You make a bad grade on
a test.

Your pet dies.

You have to brush your teeth
before bed.

You can't find your parent
or guardian in a store.

A stranger grabs you in a
parking lot.

You have to eat a vegetable
that you don't like.

Your house catches fire
and burns down.

Your sibling accidentally breaks
your favorite toy.

You can't find your favorite
shirt.

Falling from a high
place.

Now that you have learned about the word "trauma" and understand what it means, it probably doesn't seem so confusing and scary. You probably have a little more courage than you did before. That's because courage comes from understanding. The more you understand, the more courage you will have!

Are there any other words or concepts related to your trauma that you don't understand? Are there any that you would like to learn about from your helpers? Make a list of the things that you feel like you need to understand so that you can have more courage.

- _____   - _____

- _____   - _____

- _____   - _____

- _____   - _____

- _____   - _____

- _____   - _____

- _____   - _____

- _____   - _____

Show this list to one of your helpers and tell them that you want to understand more about your trauma. Maybe you will talk about some of them; maybe you will look some of them up; or maybe you will learn about some of them in stories. With all your questions answered and your understanding clearer than it was before, you will have to courage you need when the time comes!

Knowledge Is Power

Like you learned in the last activity, a trauma can change us and make it difficult to get back to the way we were before. A trauma can make us nervous, interrupt our thoughts, or make our bodies do things that we feel like we can't control. It can also make us feel sad, angry, or scared for a long time. It is hard to feel the way we did before, especially when our thoughts seem so out of control. Sometimes, we can even feel like we are crazy... but that's not true! The way you have been feeling since your trauma is normal. That is what is supposed to happen to us after a trauma.

Complete a picture of yourself below that shows how you have been feeling since your trauma happened.

Have you ever built a snowman or had a snowball fight? If so, you probably picked up a wad of snow, packed it tight, then started adding snow to it. You watched it grow and grow until it was just the right size you needed.

If you keep packing snow, the snowball keeps growing. If the snowball somehow got away from you and rolled down a hill, it would keep growing and growing until it reached the bottom of the hill and stopped rolling. Our worries can sometimes get away from us just like a snowball rolling down a hill. Our worries can grow and grow until they take up all the room in our heads. Also, each time we worry about something not worth worrying about, we are packing snow onto the snowball. While some worrying is appropriate, the challenge is to stop worrying about what it's silly to worry about—stop packing snow when we don't have to. In order to control the space in our heads, we have to learn to control our worries. This means that we have to realize a few things:

- That worrying is completely normal, but
- That we can control our worrying by not packing snow when we don't have to, and
- That we can learn to tell the difference between when to pack snow and when not to.

Let's start understanding our worry by looking at the emotions it causes. See if you can tell which emotions make up the snowball below. Write down each emotion you can recognize and then pair each emotion with the worries that cause it.

I.8 Look How Far You've Come! CAPABLE, COURAGE

You have come such a long way! Let's look at what you have learned from each activity.

I.1   You learned **to show a new helper who you are!**

I.2   You learned **that you have excellent helpers in your family!**

I.3   You learned **that you have even more helpers in your community!**

I.4   You learned **what the word "trauma" means!**

I.5   You learned **what other confusing words mean!**

I.6   You learned that, **even though you're having trouble, you aren't crazy!**

I.7   You learned about **your worries and the emotions they can make you feel!**

I.8   You learned **how far you have come!**

What else have you learned? (Don't be afraid to ask a helper to help with this part.)

_____

_____

_____

_____

_____

_____

_____

_____

_____

_____

 Gaining Ground

11

Therapeutic Stage II — Assessment & Identification

By this point in the therapeutic relationship, the bridge between you and the client should be in place and you should have some substantial understanding of your client as an individual, the events that led to therapy, and their perspective of themselves and their family, the abuse, and you. During this therapeutic stage, the primary focus is clinical assessment and the identification of presenting problems. Conduct formal and informal assessments that probe for problem behaviors, irrational beliefs or skewed perspectives, and social and familial context. Be prepared to articulate your clinical impressions, to investigate probable diagnoses, and to formulate a robust treatment plan. Like a detective, you will investigate and follow leads until you are prepared to build a case—the treatment plan.

Following Adlerian treatment protocols, the clinician would assess family atmosphere, birth order, early and/or suppressed recollections, personality profiles (of both the client and her/his family members), and daily life skills functioning. The task of this stage is to determine and understand the client's view of self, others, and the world—specifically around the parameters of the Crucial C's. In assessing the client's view of others and the world, some views might range from coherent and organized to incoherent and disorganized or from warm and accepting to cold and rigid.

In assessing the client's view of self according to the Crucial C's, determine the client's feelings about each of the following questions:

- **Connect . . . . "Do I experience love and belongingness?"**

- **Count . . . . . . "Do I feel significant and important?"**

- **Courage . . . . "Do I have a strong enough sense of self to meet challenges?"**

- **Capable . . . . "Do I have strengths, talents, and assets?"**

It is around these attributes, according to Adler, that an individual's sense of encouragement (adjustment) develops. Without a solid sense of each Crucial C, individuals become discouraged and symptomatology worsens.

Adler deduced four personality profiles from what he theorized to be four primary priorities. In his view, each individual strives for one of four primary goals, and referred to these goals as priorities. Knowing the personality priority of an individual can tell us much about their view of the world, what they want from others, and how they attempt to get it. The prescription below each personality priority suggests how to build rapport and work effectively with a client of each type. They are as follows:

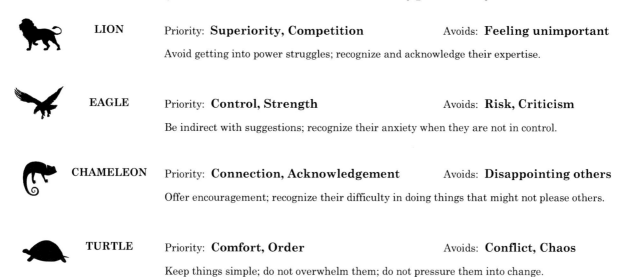

LION   Priority: **Superiority, Competition**   Avoids: **Feeling unimportant**

Avoid getting into power struggles; recognize and acknowledge their expertise.

EAGLE   Priority: **Control, Strength**   Avoids: **Risk, Criticism**

Be indirect with suggestions; recognize their anxiety when they are not in control.

CHAMELEON   Priority: **Connection, Acknowledgement**   Avoids: **Disappointing others**

Offer encouragement; recognize their difficulty in doing things that might not please others.

TURTLE   Priority: **Comfort, Order**   Avoids: **Conflict, Chaos**

Keep things simple; do not overwhelm them; do not pressure them into change.

Be sure to integrate into the treatment process the priorities and aversions motivating your client according to their personality profile. This knowledge can be very helpful in understanding an individual's overarching desires, fears, frustrations, and how the individual gains a feeling of significance; it can also provide an excellent starting place in the approximation of a client's perspective. Understanding Adler's personality profiles can also aid you in approaching the client's family members, teachers, or other professionals with whom you must consult regarding the client's treatment.

A brief note of caution: remember that personality typologies are conceptual tools and not holistic descriptions or diagnostic summaries of the client. Each person is a unique being with a unique set of perspectives, traits, and experiences, and cannot be reduced to a personality profile. Rather, use these profiles to promote insight into and discussion about your client's motivations, goals, and private logic.

This therapeutic stage concludes with two clinical accomplishments: (1) approximation of the client's private logic, and (2) the formulation of a treatment plan. Once you have assessed the client's worldview and have gained some understanding of her or his family and social atmosphere, you should come to approximate and adopt the client's private logic. "Private logic" is the Adlerian term given to what broader views might call the client's phenomenology or point of reference. It is a view colored by the client's beliefs, experiences, desires, fears, and ongoing relationships. Private logic is the ubiquitous schema through which the client interprets incoming information.

By the end of this therapeutic stage, your thorough assessment of the client's perspective, experiences, and situation should provide you with sufficient information, combined with your own clinical insights, to create a treatment plan. Clinical studies nearly unanimously demonstrate that, in addition to other indicators such as quality of the therapeutic relationship, client mindfulness, and readiness to change, the degree of collaboration with the client during treatment planning foreshadows successful psychotherapy (Adler, 1928; Kottman, 2003; Prochaska & DiClemente, 1983; Yalom, 2009). This workbook offers the client an opportunity to participate in treatment planning; this opportunity follows activities that foster self-understanding so that the client can, indeed, participate in an informed manner. Furthermore, recall that treatment plans are not static, but dynamic. Be prepared and encouraged to revise the treatment plan as the therapeutic relationship progresses and new strengths, challenges, insights, and goals emerge.

Note that, for these assessments, we will diverge from a purist Adlerian perspective for the purposes of diagnosis and in acknowledgement of the potential for these matters to become tangible beyond the therapeutic session (i.e., courts of law, social services, collaboration with other professionals, etc.). Remember, also, that families cannot be clinically diagnosed, only clinically described.

There are many different types of animals in the world. Each type of animal has or does something that makes it unique and unlike the others. Even though each animal type is different from the others, there is one thing that binds them all together—they are all trying to survive with the unique traits they each have. Some animals use strength and force to survive, some use agility and cunning, some use camouflage, and others use armor.

Which animal are you most like? How do you survive? When you are threatened, do you try to overpower the situation? When you are intimidated, do you try to find a way to get control? When you are nervous around someone, do you do things you normally wouldn't do so that they like you? When you are upset, do you bottle up and shut down? Don't be afraid to ask your helpers which one they think you are. They might not be right, but it surely will help you figure out which animal you are most like.

LION   Uses <u>strength</u> and <u>force</u> to survive

Lions are competitive and like to know that they are winners.

EAGLE   Uses <u>agility</u> and <u>cunning</u> to survive

Eagles like be in control and for others to know they are smart.

CHAMELEON   Uses <u>camouflage</u> to survive

Chameleons change their colors to make other people happy with them.

TURTLE   Uses <u>armor</u> to survive

Turtles enjoy feeling comfortable and protected from difficult things.

On one of the next four pages, find the animal that you are most like and color it any way you want! You could even draw your own version of that animal. What would you look like if you were that animal? When you are finished, keep your animal. You could pin it on the refrigerator, hang it up in your room, glue a popsicle stick to the back and make it into a puppet, or leave it with a helper. This way, you'll have your animal if you ever need it remember how you survive or to play a character in a story.

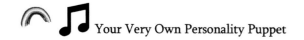

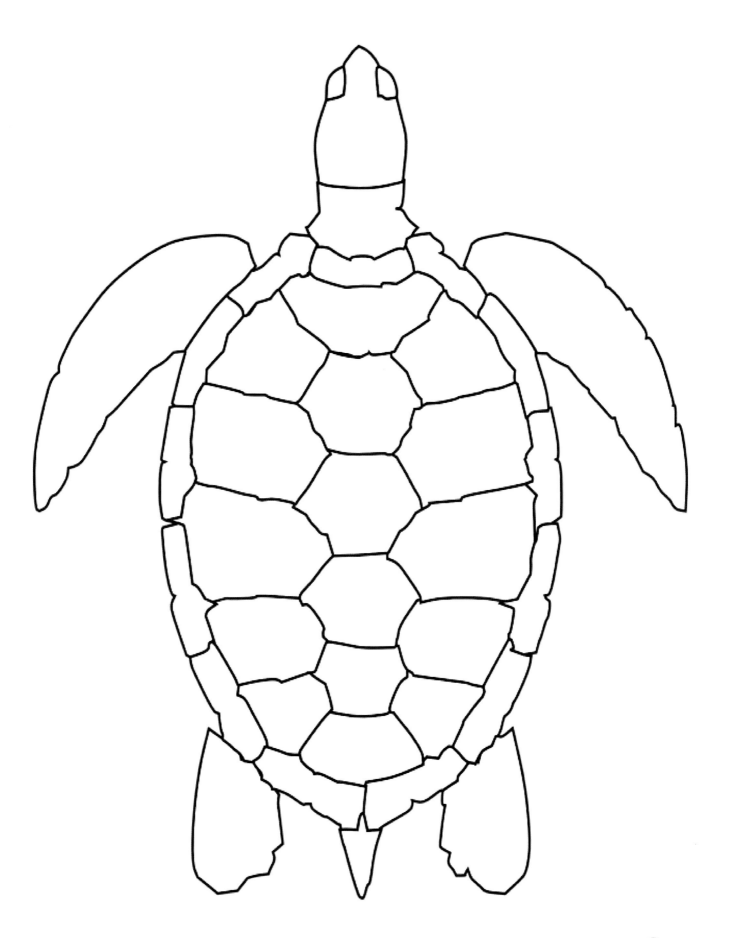

Even though a trauma makes us feel sad, angry, or scared, we do not have to feel this way forever. It will take hard work and courage, but it is possible to heal and grow after a trauma! This is what your helpers want to help you do.

Suppose we had a magic wand that could make your trauma disappear, just like that! After we waved the wand, how would you notice that the magic is working? What would be different? Draw a picture below of what will be different about you and your life after healing from your trauma. Be sure to include yourself in your picture!

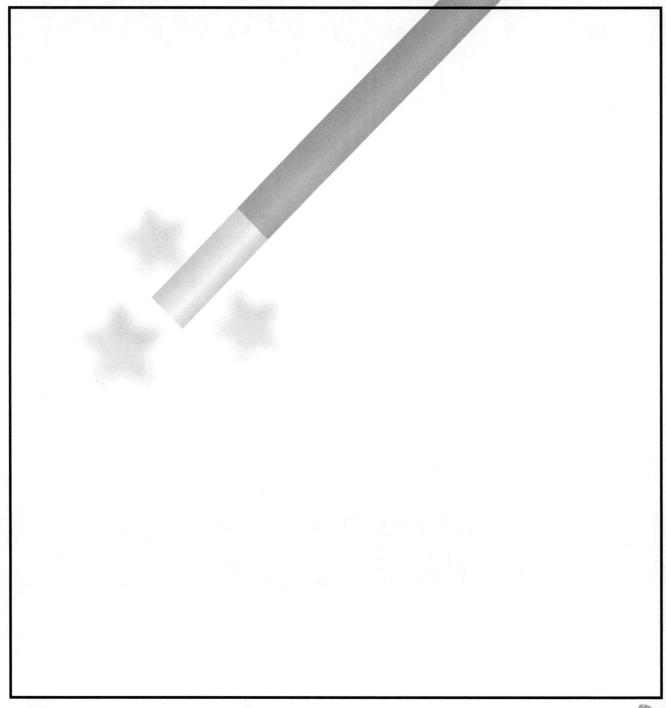

II.3   I've Got Pride!

Do you know what being proud feels like? It's that really good feeling we get when we have or do something good that we want other people to know about. Everyone has something to be proud of—even if it being proud that they are a unique individual. When we have things to be proud of and we know what those things are, it helps us to be strong. This is called recognizing our strengths! You'll find that this can help you through some pretty tough situations. So, what are some of the things you're proud of?

I am proud of being _____.

I am proud of doing _____.

I am proud of having _____.

I am proud of knowing_____.

Now, circle the things you're proud of!

SCHOOL

ATHLETICS

CREATIVITY

HELPING

RELIGION

PETS

FAMILY

CHORES

Last, draw one thing you're really proud of!

 Empty Box

Have you ever wondered why someone in your life behaves the way they do? Have you seen someone do something that didn't make sense and wondered what was going on inside that person? Have you ever wondered why *you* behave the way you do? Well you can look inside yourself and search for the answers to those questions. Looking for inside answers is called **INTROSPECTION**. When we look inside ourselves, we rarely get the answers as quickly as we would sometimes like. Introspection takes time and very careful thought. When we get really good at introspection, we get to know ourselves better and better. We can learn what scares us, what makes us happy, what makes us angry, and what makes us sad. Through introspection, we become experts on ourselves.

Do you remember the Play Prescription called "Knowledge Is Power?" It explained that the more we know about something, the more control we have when reacting to it. This works even with ourselves! The more we learn about ourselves, the better we can control ourselves and our reactions to the things that make us scared, happy, angry, and sad. Power over ourselves is the goal and introspection is how we get it! So, how do we look inside? Let's start simple. Try answering the questions below about what causes you to have certain emotions and why. The "Why?" is the hard part; it should take some time if you are doing it right. Think hard and don't be afraid to share your thoughts with a helper. They can help you make sense of your own thoughts. The perspective of others can even help you understand yourself, because sometimes they know things about you that you don't even know about yourself.

What is one thing that makes you SCARED? _____.

Why? _____

_____

What is one thing that makes you HAPPY? _____.

Why? _____

_____

What is one thing that makes you ANGRY? _____.

Why? _____

_____

What is one thing that makes you SAD? _____.

Why? _____

_____

Soon, you will be able to introspect about much more complicated things!

 Emotions Chart

24

Since you've had some practice answering some simple questions about your emotions, you may be ready to introspect a little deeper. Fear can make us do some strange things. Fear can make us want to shut down. It can paralyze us. It can even take control of our decisions. When we are full of fear, we can make decisions about our lives *based* on that fear instead of what we really want or what is best for us. Fear can make us become somebody we don't like being. It can make us hurt others, or even hurt ourselves unknowingly. Through introspection, we can better understand our fears and better control our reactions to them. Soon enough, we can take back control of our lives and our decisions.

Think about what scares you most. What are the things that paralyze you or make you want to shut down? Surely you can think of a few things that scare you like this? If not, ask a helper to sort through your thoughts with you. Just like in the last activity, the "because" part is the hardest and will take the most time and the most courage. You have learned a lot about yourself so far, so you have the courage to do this!

_____ **scares me**

because _____

_____ .

_____ **scares me**

because _____

_____ .

_____ **scares me**

because _____

_____ .

_____ **scares me**

because _____

_____ .

_____ **scares me**

because _____

_____ .

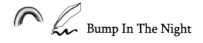

Several Asian cultures have a view of people as capable of both good and bad behaviors. They believe that the forces of good and bad live within each of us and they call those forces "Yin" and "Yang." The symbol below is what they use of represent those forces within us. Notice how the white ("good") and the gray ("bad") interlock inside a single circle? This is how they represent good and bad within the same person.

In the white spaces, write good things that you do. In the gray spaces, write some of the things you do that might not be so good. It's all right to have things in *both* of these spaces because, remember, each person is capable of both good and bad.

As good as you have become at introspection, you can still learn about yourself from others. Other people have a perspective of you, so they might notice things about you that you don't notice. They may also understand things that you don't or can't yet understand. What can you learn about your behavior from other people in your life? What would other people say about your bad behavior? Is there anything that your family members, teachers, or anybody else has noticed that you could do better? Anything that you get into trouble for doing over and over again?

Below, fill in the speech bubbles beside each figure. Write what you have heard at least three people in your life say that you do 'wrong' or could do better. Make two of them family members and the other one someone from school. Here is an example: Mom, Grandpa, a Teacher.

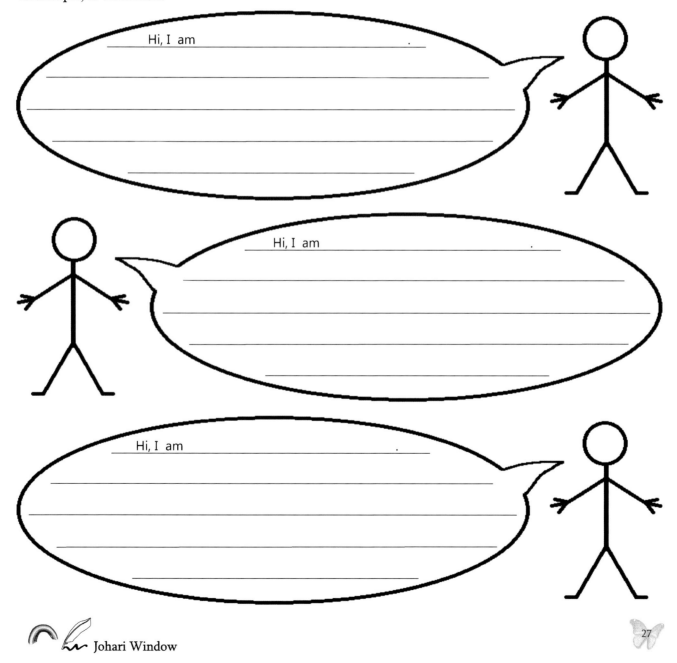

Johari Window

Yet again, let's take a moment to look at how far you have come and how much you have learned!

II.1   You learned **what you use to survive and what animal you are most like!**

II.2   You learned **what you would like to change in your life!**

II.3   You learned **that you have many things to be proud of!**

II.4   You learned **how to introspect!**

II.5   You learned **about your own fears!**

II.6   You learned **that it is normal to do both good and bad things!**

II.7   You learned **to consider things about yourself that other people can see!**

Now let's learn something else—a mantra! A mantra is a short, memorable statement that we can repeat to ourselves. It can remind us of who we are when times get tough. A mantra works best when you create it yourself. A good way to create your own mantra is to think of your three favorite things about yourself and simply put them into a sentence. Below, list as many things that you like about yourself or things that make you unique. Then, choose three and place them into your mantra and practice saying it aloud. A mantra can be especially helpful when rehearsed in front of a mirror. Try it!

_____ _____ _____

_____ _____ _____

_____ _____ _____

_____ _____ _____

_____ _____ _____

"*I am* _____ ,

I am _____ ,

and I am _____ ."

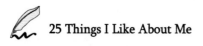

Therapeutic Stage III — Treatment

In this third therapeutic stage, the clinician should have already solidified some clinical impressions of the client, family context, and situation. A treatment plan should also be in place by this point. Bear in mind, however, that the best treatment plans are dynamic instruments, rather than static. The clinician should also, as part of the therapeutic process, have made effort to set therapeutic goals in collaboration with the client (and the family, if applicable). Prioritize the client's presenting problems as based on *severity*, by which is meant the degree of interruption of successful and adaptive capability to function in important dimensions of daily life. In order to ensure a stable and sustaining treatment environment, the sexually abused client's major presenting problems need to be brought under control and the client may need to be stabilized within herself or himself (intrapersonally), among family (interpersonally), and at school, work, and peers (vocationally and socially), as applicable. For example, an unruly and eruptive client will need to be stabilized at a behavioral level first so that she or he does not lose access to therapy due to forced relocation, juvenile detention or incarceration, or loss of legal transportation. With successful and accurate prioritization of the client's presenting problems, the clinician will contribute to the likelihood that the client will be able to remain in treatment once treatment commences.

From the Adlerian perspective, individuals are not pathological but are, instead, *discouraged*. This term, in its Adlerian context, refers to one of two responses to feelings of inferiority—the other being inspiration. Discouragement is brought about by the ever-present "discrepancy between the self-perception and the self-ideal; it provokes either forfeit or overcompensation" (Kottman, 2003, p. 25). Discouraged individuals struggle to get their needs met, as based upon their personality profiles and those of the people nearest them. This approach operates from Adler's theory of Individual Psychology. This phenomenological approach—based on the client's lived experiences, perceptions, needs, desires, and expectations—respects the client's 'own truth' (private logic). The clinician "helps the [client] replace private logic with common sense" (Kottman, 2003, p. 221).

Sexually abused clients can also be addressed through a prescriptive, integrative stance utilizing other theoretical perspectives and models. Maslow's Hierarchy of Needs, for instance, would reveal that sexually abused clients, as most others, have unmet need at some level. Erikson's Psychosocial Stages, similarly, demonstrate that these clients have not yet completed one stage or more; their life tasks have been truncated by trauma. While these and other theories all insinuate that the trauma is experienced on multiple interior and exterior fronts—physical, mental/psychological, emotional, and spiritual violations—Adlerian play therapy speaks uniquely to the treatment of trauma by identifying, addressing, and resolving all aspects of the trauma in an effort to assist the client to approximate a return to pre-trauma functioning.

Treatment is the portion of the therapeutic process wherein the clinician will systematically implement the different components of the treatment plan as well as isolate and address different aspects of the client's presenting problems. Confronting the issues and achieving catharsis are the major themes of this therapeutic stage. Van der Kolk, McFarlane, & Weisaeth (1996) suggested that treatment should "address the twin issues of helping patients (1) regain a sense of safety in their bodies and (2) complete the unfinished past" (p. 17). This view is particularly helpful, as victims of sexual abuse most often have suffered some bodily transgression and consequent truncation of development. Some stage is incomplete.

Norton's 4 S's is a clinical model that condensed the healing process of sexually abused clients into four stages: **Sensory, Soma, Surge, and Soothe** (Norton & Norton, 2006). The stages may be described as follows:

- **Sensory** — visual, auditory, tactile, olfactory, taste, and motor sensations trigger recall of sensations associated with the trauma during the course of play; the clinician should lend special attention to expressions beyond the verbal level (grunts, groans, growls, etc.) to note the deep interiority of the experience the client is undergoing; energy and tension associated with the recall of the trauma accumulate in the client's body;

- **Soma** — physiological, somatic memories resulting in inadequate processing of trauma manifest during the course of play without integrating affective and sensory-motor elements;
- **Surge** — discharge of trauma energy in safe, permissive modality and environment (expressions in this stage can differ according to gender and can rightly be quite aggressive and seem out-of-control); facilitation of the completion and reorientation of trauma responses allowing for successful flight-or-flight, thus, ending the arrest associate with the original trauma; and
- **Soothe** — normalization and self-regulation; return to some form of pre-trauma function; reclaiming of self.

(Norton, Ferriegel, & Norton, 2011)

Victims of sexual abuse cycle through the first three stages more frequently than they reach the last stage. The environment fostered by the therapeutic relationship and the play space serves as the catalyst, ensuring that the client can reach the final (healing) stage with greater occasion (Norton, Ferriegel, & Norton, 2011).

Two important caveats to this therapeutic stage address the client's home, school or vocational, and social environments, as well as the authority figures therein. First, this workbook provides a therapeutic model that works best *following* police and social service intervention and *after* any active abuser(s) have been removed from the home environment of the client. The treatment stage can elicit such behaviors as regression, decompensation, withdrawal, and exacerbation of acting out and other problem behaviors. The clinician must be clear with the client (as well as her/his family and school officials, if the client is a minor) that behavior can worsen in this stage. Additionally, the clinician will want to alert the appropriate parties of this likelihood so that treatment is not terminated in error. A final mentionable caveat to this stage warns the clinician to recall the versatile and flexible natures of the treatment plan as a therapeutic tool. As such, it should be updated to reflect both client progress or regress as well as efficacy of the agencies of change employed with the client.

Not only are worries and fears normal, but anger is also perfectly normal. Anger can be healthy—if it is dealt with in healthy ways. It is an inside signal that tells us something isn't quite right. Anger is a "secondary emotion." That means that it is an emotion that *only follows* other "primary emotions" like hurt, fear, and sadness. Anger is just our way of gaining a sense of control when we feel those bad primary emotions. Since anger comes from normal things in life, anger itself is also normal! The best way to deal with anger is to look at the primary emotions that it follows.

Circle each emotion that you understand well and notice how each can lead to anger.

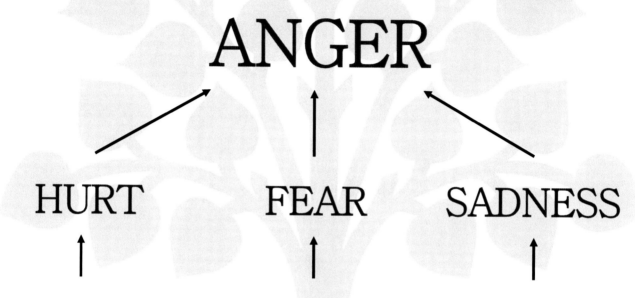

ANGER

HURT

- BETRAYAL
- MISTREATED
- DISRESPECTED
- VICTIMIZED
- VIOLATED
- INJURED
- HUMILIATED
- MISUNDERSTOOD

FEAR

- Of LOSS
- Of PAIN
- Of LONELINESS
- Of RISK
- Of VIOLENCE
- THREATENED
- VULNERABILITY
- ANXIETY

SADNESS

- LOSS
- DISAPPOINTED
- DISCOURAGED
- ISOLATED
- OSTRACISED
- ABANDONED
- REJECTED
- HOPELESS

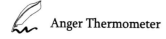 Anger Thermometer

When you get angry—really, really angry—how does it feel? Does it feel like you can't sit still? Does it feel like there is something inside you trying to get out? Does it feel like everything around you gets dark? You may fee like you have enough energy to break something or hurt someone. You may feel like you're going to burst if you don't scream. You might even forget yourself and disappear into a fit of rage.

Use your new ability of introspection to think and write about how you feel when you're really, really angry.

_____

_____

_____

_____

_____

Have you ever felt bad for something you did while you were really, really angry? Did you break something important, hurt yourself or someone else, or say something you didn't mean to someone you love? What happened? How did you feel afterward?

_____

_____

_____

_____

Our body gives us signs we can look for in order to know what we're getting really, really angry. If we know what signs to look for, we can get better at controlling our anger; and, if we can control our anger, we can stop doing things that we later regret.

• Our thoughts become very fast and they can seem unclear;

• When we talk, we start to lose control of our volume;

• Our muscles—especially in our chest and shoulders—become tighter;

• Our breathing starts to speed up;

• Our hands and feet might start to feel cold;

• We might start to sweat or feel hot; and

• We might even become tense and begin to shake.

 Five Senses Poem: Anger

Anger is an inescapable part of life. There will always be things that make us angry because there will always be things that hurt, frighten, or sadden us. Since life is full of those things and we can't do away with anger, the challenge is to learn how to handle anger in healthy ways. Some people can't deal with their anger in healthy ways because they can't even talk about it. There are a few reasons why people don't talk about their anger—some of them are true and some of them are not. See if you can tell which of the thoughts below are true and which are not. Color in *only* the thought bubbles that you think are true and good reasons not to talk about your anger.

Anger Umbrella

Emotions are a part of being human; they help make us who we are. You have the right to experience *every* emotion you could possibly ever think of. When your life makes you sad, you have the right to experience that sadness. When something makes you angry, you have the right to experience that anger. And when someone brings joy into your life, you have the right to experience that joy. You have the right to your emotions!

What you don't have the right to do is behave any way you want *because* of your emotions. You don't have the right to make someone else sad because you are sad. You don't have the right to hurt yourself, someone else, or an animal, or to destroy something valuable when you are angry. Since anger is an inescapable part of life, we have to learn how to handle it in healthy ways. Let's consider the difference between healthy and unhealthy ways to handle your anger. Circle the following ways that you think are healthy ways to deal with your anger and mark a line through the ways that you think are unhealthy.

EXERCISE   THROW THINGS ACROSS the ROOM

DISRESPECT PROPERTY of OTHERS   SPORTS

ASK for TIME ALONE   CREATIVE ARTS

HURT or INJURE SOMEONE   THROW a TANTRUM

LISTEN TO or PLAY MUSIC   SAY HATEFUL THINGS

SAFELY BREAK SOMETHING of NO VALUE   SCREAM INTO a PILLOW

DO a CALMING ROUTINE   HURT the FAMILY PET

HURT or THREATEN to HURT YOURSELF   CHORES

RUN AWAY from HOME   STEAL SOMETHING

Notice that there are just as many unhealthy ways to deal with anger as there are healthy ways. This means you must be especially careful about which ways you choose to behave when you are angry. With time and practice, you will get better at handling your anger in healthy ways.

 Bill of Behavioral Rights

Just like anger, problems will always come! They are an inescapable part of life. You've probably noticed just how true this is by now. In the same way that we must learn how to deal with anger, we must also get better at problem solving. There is more than one solution to every problem. Some of those solutions are better than the others. Sometimes, there may even be a *best* solution! But it's usually not the one that comes to mind first.

Imagine that you have to get through to the other side of a giant forest. Your first idea is likely just to walk straight through the forest. Two things happen if you go with your first idea. First, you start down a path full of problems that you can't see yet. There may be a pit of snakes or quicksand or a scary cave on the path straight through the forest. Second, you miss the opportunity to take any of the other easier paths through the forest. You forget that you could take the path over the mountain or the path around the pond. All in all, if you go with your first idea, you may have not found the *best* path to take. The key is to consider other paths besides your first idea. The best path is the one that is the easiest with the least amount of danger. See if you can find the easiest way through the forest.

When we find the best solution to a problem, we put that problem in its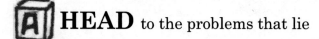

In order to find the best solution to every problem, the first thing we must do is

AUSE to give ourselves time to think of the best solution. If we rush straight to the first idea we have, we won't have time to think of anything better or consider the problems with our first idea.

The next thing to do is to 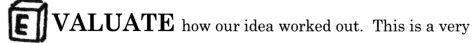**OOK** **A****HEAD** to the problems that lie between us and where we're trying to get. In looking ahead, we also take time for other ideas to come to mind—possibly even better ideas.

After we have a few ideas, we can **C****HOOSE** which idea we are going to go with. Decide which idea gives you the safest and healthiest path to the solution.

Last, we must **E****VALUATE** how our idea worked out. This is a very important part of solving problems, because there is always something to learn from today for the next time a problem comes our way!

Try identifying the steps to putting this problem in its PLACE by drawing the correct letter in each empty block. Here's the problem: *Your teacher gives you an assignment that you don't understand how to complete and has left the classroom. You must have the assignment done by the time your teacher gets back or you will be in trouble.*

 Now that you have chosen to stay in your seat, complete the assignment, and you have turned in the work you did while your teacher was gone, pay attention to how your teacher reacts to this. Did your teacher get upset with the students who did nothing? Did you get a gold star for your work? Did anyone get in trouble for leaving their seat to find the teacher?

 Take a moment; breathe in deeply and exhale slowly. There's no need to panic. Ten minutes is enough time to do this assignment.

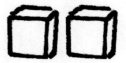 **Consider your options. You could go looking for your teacher to ask for more directions. You could do nothing and explain that you didn't do anything because you didn't understand. Or you could give it your best shot to show that you tried and, if your teacher is upset, explain that you didn't understand.**

 Decide that staying in your seat and attempting to complete the assignment is the best idea you can come up with. This way, you will not get in trouble for leaving the room and you will have at least something to turn in when your teacher returns. Begin working!

 **Bubble Breaths**

40

III.7 No Trespassing!

Have you ever had a crabby neighbor who gets upset when people go into their yard? Maybe you have lost a ball while playing and it went into their yard. When you went to get it, your neighbor yelled at you, "Get off my property!" This doesn't necessarily make your neighbor a mean person; they have the right to ask you to leave. They own the property and they don't have to let anyone in the yard that they don't want to.

Your personal space, your body, and your mind is like your yard—YOU own it! You get to decide who gets to be in your personal space, who gets to see or touch your body, and who gets to know what's on your mind. These are your rights! The thing about having rights, though, is that you are not the only one who has them. Other people have these exact same rights; you have to respect their rights just like you want them to respect your rights.

If your personal space, your body, and your mind are like your home and yard, color the areas that represent those things. The areas that you color should represent the spaces where YOU get to decide who gets in. However, the areas that you leave uncolored are the areas that you have to respect for other people.

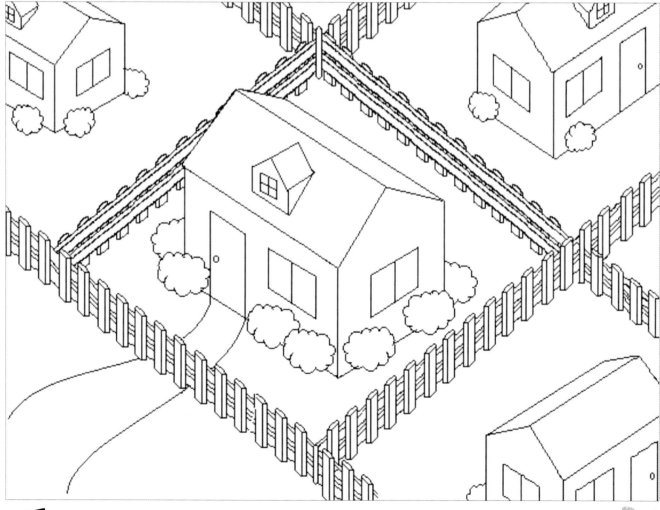

♫ Space Invaders

We are all human, and human beings are social beings. This means that we are meant to have bonds and relationships with other people. We are not meant to live our lives alone in silence. We are meant to share our burdens and our troubles, because sometimes life can be too hard to handle on our own. Human beings also have the gift of language! Language lets us share our thoughts and ideas as well as to explain to others how we feel. What a wonderful gift to waste when we keep the things that trouble us to ourselves! Don't you think we should use our gift to the fullest? Don't you think that we should talk about what's bothering us? This is one of the most important ways that human beings strengthen their bonds with one another. It's practically what makes us human!

Think of a time when you finally talked about something that had been bothering you. You probably felt better almost immediately. Suddenly, somebody else knew about what was bothering you and you weren't dealing with it alone anymore. It is like something really heavy—something that is weighing you down, and holding you back—is taken off your back and you can walk free again. Sometimes, talking about mixed up feelings and thoughts can actually help us see them more clearly for ourselves. Talking really helps!

Describe a time when you finally used your human gift and talked about something that had been weighing you down. Who did you tell? How did you tell them? How did you feel after you told them?

_____

_____

_____

_____

_____

_____

_____

_____

_____

How Does The Closet Feel?

Did you know that there are two kinds of secrets? There are good secrets and bad secrets. Look at these lists of things about good and bad secrets.

GOOD SECRETS	BAD SECRETS
Usually about something surprising or fun	Usually about something bad or wrong
Give us positive feelings	Makes us scared, nervous, or guilty
Are meant to be told someday	Are never meant to be told

Can you think of an example of each kind of secret? Start by writing out the secret. Then, for each secret, write out whether it was about something fun or something wrong, what kind of feelings the secret gave you, and whether it was okay to tell the secret.

GOOD SECRET	BAD SECRET

When you are asked to keep a bad secret, tell someone who can help you! Once you know the difference between good and bad secrets, it will be much easier to know when you should tell someone. This will help you recognize when you are in a bad secret situation and get you out of it sooner. It will even help you avoid them entirely.

You may have learned about your five senses in school: sight, sound, taste, smell, and touch. These are the ways that our brains use our bodies to take in information about the world we live in. They serve many purposes; the most important reason for our senses is to keep us alive and healthy. For example, when you see a bright-colored insect, you probably realize pretty quickly that it is dangerous; when you hear a dog growling, you probably know better than to try to pet it; or when you touch something hot, you probably don't get very close to it again. The last example was an example of how our sense of touch keeps us safe. We experience pain so that we can know when we are in danger of bodily harm. We also feel pleasure and comfort so that we can know when we are safe. Touch is a complicated sense! It can make us smile, it can make us scream or cry, and it can make us feel icky inside. Feeling icky inside is a way that our brains let us know that we are uncomfortable or in danger. This kind of touch may not hurt necessarily, but your brain still knows that something is wrong. Usually, someone or something has come into your personal space without your permission.

A touch that makes us smile and relax is **<u>SOOTHING</u>**, and can makes us feel

HAPPY   ECSTATIC   SILLY   RELAXED

A touch that makes us scream or cry is **<u>HURTFUL</u>**, and can makes us feel

SAD   HURT   ANGRY

A touch that makes us feel icky inside is **<u>INAPPROPRIATE</u>**, and can makes us feel

EMBARRASSED   SHOCKE   CONFUSED   PARALYZED   TERROR

Have you ever experienced an inappropriate touch? If so, how did it make you feel?

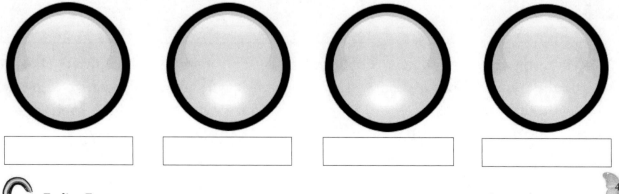

Feeling Faces

Now that you understand the difference between the three kinds of touches and the feelings that each touch causes, you will probably find it easier to tell the touches apart in this exercise. Think about each event on the left and the feeling it would give most people. Then draw the face of that feeling in the blank face. Last, circle the kind of touch you think the event describes.

A kid on the playground
knocks you down

SOOTHING
HURTFUL
INAPPROPRIATE

Your parents stroke your
back as you fall asleep

SOOTHING
HURTFUL
INAPPROPRIATE

Someone touches your private area
and asks you not to tell anyone

SOOTHING
HURTFUL
INAPPROPRIATE

Your friend gives you a 'high five'

SOOTHING
HURTFUL
INAPPROPRIATE

You get a spanking for
misbehaving at home

SOOTHING
HURTFUL
INAPPROPRIATE

A person kisses you after you
told them they could not

SOOTHING
HURTFUL
INAPPROPRIATE

SOOTHING TOUCHES

- Identify people, things, and places that make us feel safe and healthy.
- Include things like pats of the head, kisses on the cheek, and hugs.
- You should celebrate and appreciate them!

HURTFUL TOUCHES

- Cause us pain, teach us, and warn us that we are in danger.
- Include things like violence, injury, or discipline from your parents.
- You should avoid them when possible and learn from them!

INAPPROPRIATE TOUCHES

- Make us feel icky inside because something is happening that we do not want to happen. These can be any body area.
- Include things like others touching us where they should not or asking us to touch them where we should not.
- You should tell an adult about them as soon as possible!

Generally, it is safe for someone to touch children in these places. It is okay for most adults to hold your hand, pat you on the head, touch your shoulder to get your attention, or tickle your feet. Notice that these areas are the furthest away from the center of your body. These areas are usually safe to touch because they are the parts that interact most with the world and other people. However, if you prefer not to be touched at all in those areas, you have a right to tell others that and demand respect for your personal boundaries!

These areas are a little more private and sensitive. It is usually alright for a trusted friend or adult to touch a child in these areas. Someone might pick you up by the waist, tap your knee to get your attention, or touch your face if you let them. Notice that these areas are closer to the center of your body. They are sensitive because they are closer to our vital organs that keep us alive.

The only people who are allowed to touch these areas are yourself, a loving parent or guardian, and the doctor. These are the most sensitive areas on our body and there is no reason that friends or other adults should touch you there or ask you to touch them there.

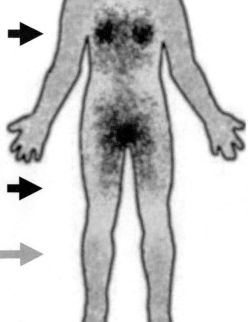

Use your new understanding of the different kinds of touch to describe your very own experiences of touch. For each area of the body below, write about a memory you have of being touched there, what kind of touch it was, and the feelings it caused you to have.

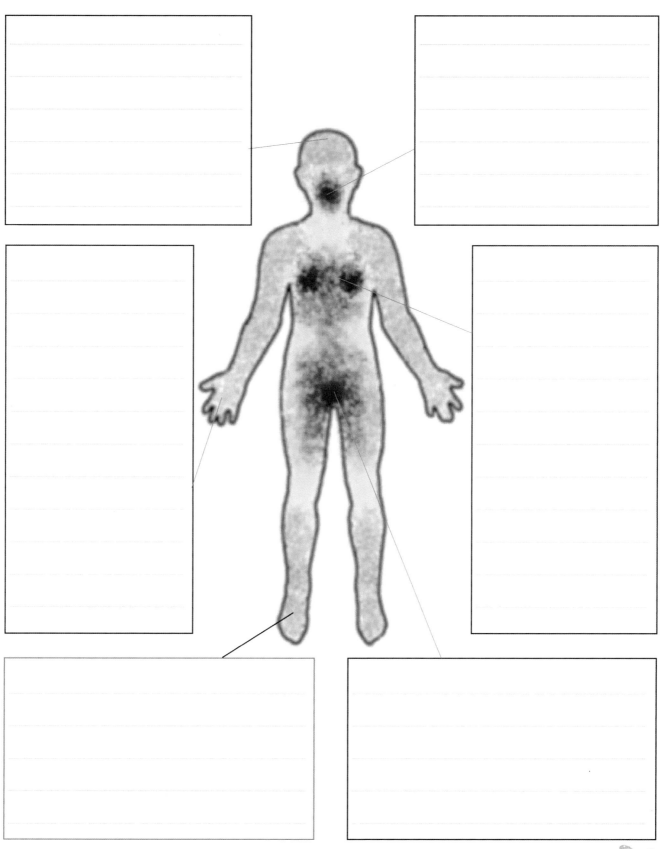

What happens when someone touches us inappropriately? When our body experiences pain that we cannot stop? When we cannot get out of a scary situation? Our brain and our body have been working together since before we were even born. They have a long history of helping one another out. When our body is under too much stress, our brain can try to protect us by making us forget where we are or what is going on. Sometimes this can cause us to feel like we cannot remember what happened. Let's call this a "retreat." Retreat means to withdraw, to pull back, to shrink or get smaller in some way. Some people retreat just a little bit—losing focus of what is happening. Other people retreat a lot—losing all memory of time and place. When we retreat from what is going on, it means that whatever was going on that made us retreat must have been really bad. Some people believe that, if you can remember how you felt when the really bad thing happened, you might be able to remember some details about what happened.

Can you remember if your brain helped you retreat? If you did, can you remember how much you retreated? How big you felt inside your head? Where it felt like you were inside your body, if anywhere at all? If you have trouble remembering parts of your story, it might help to remember how you felt in your body during your story.

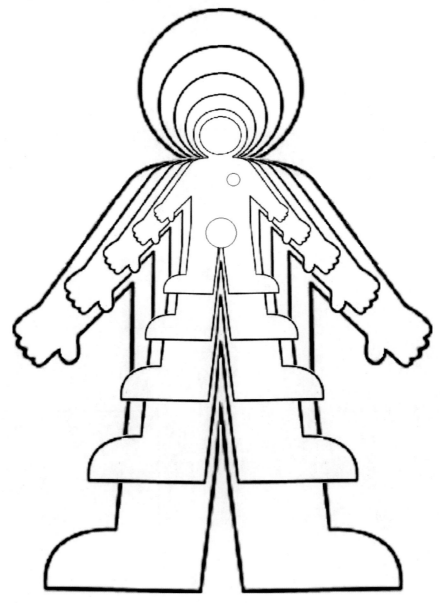

Every story has to have at least three elements: **CHARACTERS**, **SETTING**, and **PLOT**.
Can you remember these elements in your story of what happened?

CHARACTERS

People, creatures, or other forces that do things and make things happen in the story.

Who was there? Who helped? Who wasn't there?

SETTING

The time and place that the story happens.

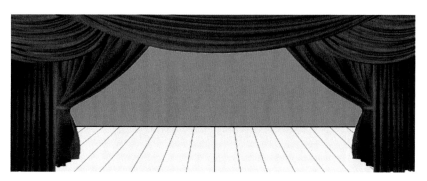

Where did your story happen? What time of year was it? What time of day was it?
Was anything else going on in your story?

PLOT

The series of events that happen in the story.

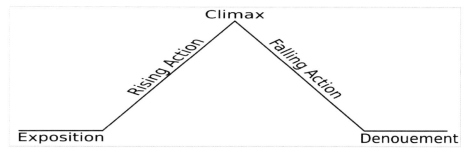

What events led up to your story? What events happened during your story?

Event Dynamics Map

Who were the **CHARACTERS** in your story?

_____

_____

_____

_____

What was the **SETTING** of your story?

_____

_____

_____

What was the **PLOT** of your story?

_____

_____

_____

_____

_____

_____

_____

_____

There are a few important things that make you *who* you are. These things include your body, your heart, and your mind. Some people would say that these are the three most important things that make you who you are. We have different levels of control over our three parts, just like the Three Little Pigs had houses made of different materials!

 **We have the least control over our body**. Not only does our body act on its own all the time, things can also happen to it that are out of our control. Our bodies are always changing, far more than our hearts and minds change. For this reason, the body is like straw—weak and flimsy when it comes to our control over it.

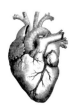 **We have a little more control over our heart**. While it can be broken by someone or make us feel certain ways we can't control, we can still control most of the thoughts that tell the heart how to feel. The heart is like sticks—strong enough to build something, but still weak when it comes to our control over it.

 We have the most control over our mind. It is true that some things can take control of our minds from us, but there are not many things that can do it. We can examine our beliefs and gain better control over our minds. While the body and the heart break easily, it takes much more to break the mind! In this way, the mind is like brick—very strong.

Color the houses below so that you can remember what your three parts are made of!

III.16 Who Is At Fault?

CAPABLE

When adults have car accidents, they have to figure out who is at fault. This means they have to find the person who did something wrong—the accident is that person's fault. In most accidents, somebody has broken a rule that caused someone else to get hurt or caused someone else's car get damaged. Somebody did something they knew better than do to. This is what it means to be at fault. In your story, inappropriate touching is the rule that someone broke and you are the one who got hurt. It can be difficult to find who is at fault in a car accident, but it is easy to find who is at fault in your story—and it isn't you! Somebody probably older and bigger then you—an adult or an older kid—did something they shouldn't have. That person's choice to break the rule caused a lot of damage.

Below, see if you can tell who is at fault in each situation. Put a check in the box for the person who is at fault in each situation.

SITUATION 1: Amy's and Cindy's mother comes home to find her favorite vase broken. Both Amy and Cindy tell their mother that they do not know who actually broke the vase. Both Cindy and Amy got grounded for being dishonest.

☐ Cindy's and Amy's mother, who left her favorite vase on the table while she was away.

☐ Cindy, who got punished alongside her sister Cindy for being dishonest.

☐ Amy, who actually broke her mother's vase and said that she didn't know who did it.

SITUATION 2: David and his brother Luke are at the grocery store with their father. They are playing in the store while their father isn't watching. Luke trips David and David falls into a shelf. David scrapes his elbow and knocks a bunch of groceries off the shelf that their father now has to pay for.

☐ David's and Luke's father, who took children into the grocery store.

☐ Luke, who tripped David and caused the groceries to fall and David to get hurt.

☐ David, who fell into the shelf and knocked all the groceries down.

SITUATION 3: Mark is taking a different path home from school than he normally does when he runs into Dudley, the class bully. Dudley pushes Mark to the ground, rips mark's shirt, and takes his lunch money for the next day. An adult comes out of a nearby house and asks what's going on. Dudley speaks up first and says that Mark fell and he was just helping Mark up. Mark is so embarrassed that he can't take up for himself and he doesn't say anything.

☐ Mark, who took a different path home from school than he normally takes.

☐ Dudley, who pushed Mark down and took his lunch money.

☐ The adult, who came out of the house after Dudley bullied Mark.

X-Ray

52

Have you ever wondered why you behave the way you do? Why other people behave the ways they do? What causes us to take one action rather than another? The answer is our beliefs and our perception! Our beliefs about ourselves, about other people, and about the world shape our perception—the way we see everything—and our perception, in turn, shapes new beliefs as they are formed. These two things—beliefs and perception—shape one another *AND* all our thoughts, feelings, and actions! If beliefs and perception are underneath all this, where do our beliefs come from? They come from our experiences—the things that have happened to us, things the we cannot change. Since we cannot change our experiences, the next most fundamental things we can change are our beliefs and perception.

But wait! Our beliefs are pretty strong, aren't they? That's why they are called "beliefs," after all. They aren't easy to change. It takes work to change a belief; and not *all* of them *can* be changed. You might be wondering *how* we can change our beliefs. We have to challenge them and dispute them. This means that, sometimes, we have to look at our beliefs and make sure that they are still true. Like old software sometimes needs new updates, our beliefs need to be checked from time to time so that we can be sure they are up to date and giving us a healthy perception of ourselves, others, and the world. Challenging our beliefs is like a software update for our brains. Our brains are like the computer and our behavior is like *what the computer does* because of the software in it. With the best software updates, we can have better perception, thoughts, feelings, and behaviors. Here is what the order looks like:

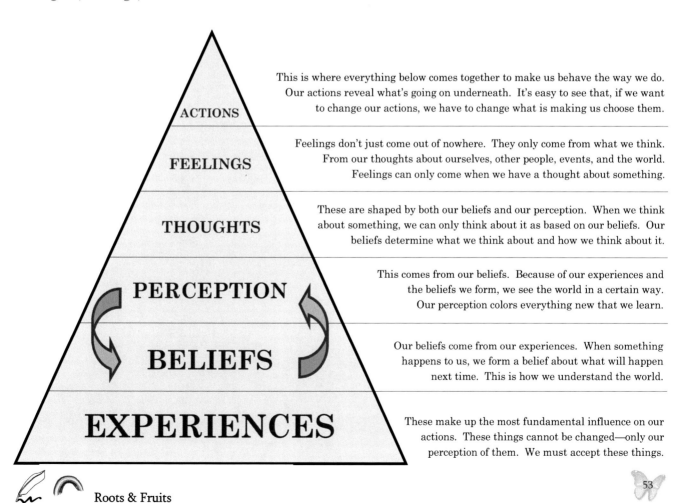

ACTIONS — This is where everything below comes together to make us behave the way we do. Our actions reveal what's going on underneath. It's easy to see that, if we want to change our actions, we have to change what is making us choose them.

FEELINGS — Feelings don't just come out of nowhere. They only come from what we think. From our thoughts about ourselves, other people, events, and the world. Feelings can only come when we have a thought about something.

THOUGHTS — These are shaped by both our beliefs and our perception. When we think about something, we can only think about it as based on our beliefs. Our beliefs determine what we think about and how we think about it.

PERCEPTION — This comes from our beliefs. Because of our experiences and the beliefs we form, we see the world in a certain way. Our perception colors everything new that we learn.

BELIEFS — Our beliefs come from our experiences. When something happens to us, we form a belief about what will happen next time. This is how we understand the world.

EXPERIENCES — These make up the most fundamental influence on our actions. These things cannot be changed—only our perception of them. We must accept these things.

Now that you know where your actions come from, let's do a little more comparison with computers. This should help you remember what you just learned for a long time! Our experiences are like the basic hardware. You can add to it, but you can't change it too much or the computer wouldn't work anymore. When we put hardware and software together, we get a function. A function is something that the computer does for us; it is the only reason for having a computer. The function is like our actions and our behavior. If we want to change the function of a computer, we can change the software on it.

Before, we saw that the software on a computer is like our brains—including our beliefs, our perception, our thoughts, and our feelings. The software is what tells a computer to do, what function to perform. There are many types of software. It comes in different programs. Some programs are for anger, some are for love, and some are for happiness. There is a software program for every single thing we do. There is also good software and bad software. Good software gives us the ability to see truth and to think clearly; bad software distorts our perception of truth and makes it difficult to think clearly. Remember that our feelings and actions follow our thoughts. Bad software makes us act in ways that are not based on truth. It can make us feel and do a lot of bad things that we wouldn't otherwise have to feel or wouldn't otherwise do. Good software, on the other hand, helps us act based on the truth, on what's real. When we are acting based on the truth, a lot of bad feelings and thoughts go away. We might be having bad feelings and choosing bad actions for no reason at all if we aren't seeing and thinking clearly.

To change your behavior, start by finding the bad software, the beliefs that need to be challenged and disputed. Then, evaluate them alone or with someone's help to see if they are still true. You may find that some are no longer true and that you don't have as many negative emotions or do as many bad things anymore. Here's an example (start at the bottom):

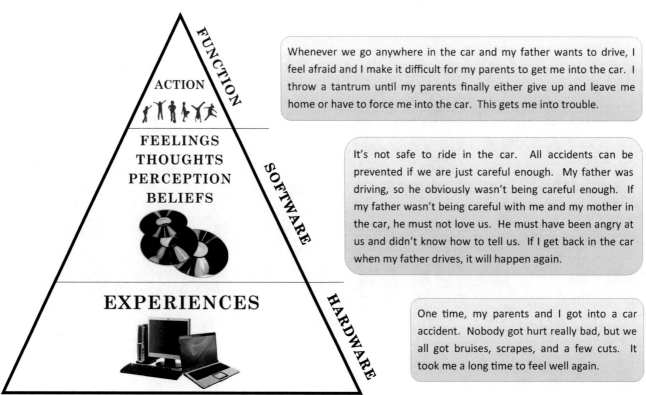

FUNCTION
ACTION

FEELINGS
THOUGHTS
PERCEPTION
BELIEFS

SOFTWARE

EXPERIENCES

HARDWARE

Whenever we go anywhere in the car and my father wants to drive, I feel afraid and I make it difficult for my parents to get me into the car. I throw a tantrum until my parents finally either give up and leave me home or have to force me into the car. This gets me into trouble.

It's not safe to ride in the car. All accidents can be prevented if we are just careful enough. My father was driving, so he obviously wasn't being careful enough. If my father wasn't being careful with me and my mother in the car, he must not love us. He must have been angry at us and didn't know how to tell us. If I get back in the car when my father drives, it will happen again.

One time, my parents and I got into a car accident. Nobody got hurt really bad, but we all got bruises, scrapes, and a few cuts. It took me a long time to feel well again.

See if you can track down bad software. Try starting with a bad behavior of yours and trace it back to bad feelings, thoughts, or beliefs. Then, try tracing it back even further to an experience that started it all. Write these things in the diagram. Ask for help if you need it! See if you can match:

- ACTION ⟶ FUNCTION,
- FEELING, THOUGHT or BELIEF ⟶ SOFTWARE, and
- EXPERIENCE ⟶ HARDWARE.

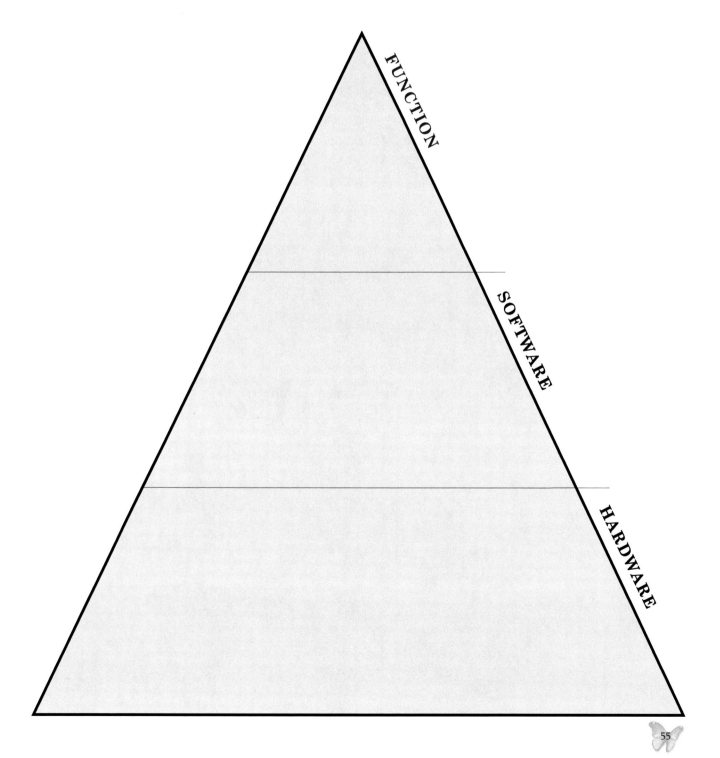

Now that you have seen how important our beliefs are, you are on your way to having more control over your thoughts, feelings, and actions. What does it look like to dispute your own beliefs? It looks like arguing with yourself. Usually we can find clues that there is a flaw in our beliefs when we others point out that we behave badly, when we have too many negative thoughts and emotions, or when we get a clue that our actions aren't making sense to others. This might look like getting in trouble at home or at school all the time, feeling sad or scared or angry all the time, or when everyone else around us believes or understands something we don't. These are clues!

What do we do when we suspect a flaw? Identify the belief and start to question it. If it falls apart when we question it, the belief was no good. If it doesn't fall apart, then it is a good belief to keep for now. We only want to keep the best ones, the ones that can't be disputed.

Find a belief that you suspect may have a flaw. If you can't, use the belief from the last activity. List that belief at the top, then ask questions about all parts of the belief, including the behavior it creates and the experience it comes from. Can you come to any conclusion? Feel encouraged to ask others for help in disputing the beliefs you suspect have flaws.

BELIEF

QUESTIONS ABOUT BEHAVIOR IT CREATES

QUESTIONS ABOUT EXPERIENCE IT COMES FROM

GENERAL QUESTIONS

CONCLUSIONS

 Eggshells

You probably know well that plants need water and sunlight in order to grow. Plants don't just soak up water and sunlight to come to them. That's only one way they get what they need. Nor do they only get what someone brings to them. That's just another way. The last way plants get what they need is to get it themselves! Despite their appearance, plants sometimes give themselves what they need. Some plants bend and grow in odd different directions so they can get more sunlight. Some plants extend their roots to reach groundwater.

Encouragement for people is like water and sunlight to plants. We need it to grow, just like plants need water and sunlight to grow. And just like plants, we can get what we need to grow in three ways. We can simply find encouragement in our environment, by noticing the small victories in our lives. This is like when plants take what is already in the environment available to them. We can also get encouragement from others around us—parents, friends, family members, and teachers. This is like when someone brings a plant water or moves it into the sunlight. Last, we can be our own source of encouragement. We can uplift ourselves with positive thoughts and self-encouragement. This is like when a plant gets what it needs on its own. If plants can do it, so can you! In each petal, write something positive about yourself that you can tell yourself when you aren't feeling encouraged.

Person Picking An Apple From A Tree

Therapeutic Stage IV — Recovery & Maintenance

At this point, it is all right if there is still pain, brokenness, and hurt, for insight has been achieved. The previous stage likely led your client through the expulsion of the bulk, if not all, of the emotional, psychological, and physical trauma associated with the sexual abuse. The intensity has been distilled from their pain and fear; the paralysis has been overcome in their body; and the trauma has been disassociated from their identity. You have likely ushered your client back to the stage at which her or his development became truncated. In Adlerian terms, you have encouraged your client and given her or him the opportunity to regain that which was stolen and discouraged your client. What your client needs now are the tools, skills, and hope necessary to continue in their development. This final therapeutic stage, rife with celebratory and termination rituals, will center around fortification of the insight your client has gained, the application or rehearsal of the new persona your client is creating, an appreciation of the new perspective your client has come to adopt, and forgiveness—the final catharsis.

Along with everything the client has learned thus far, she or he will also need to know how to avoid being reoffended against. Your client will need to apply the new insights to the future. You will need to attend the installation of skills: vigilance, aversion, and self-care. In rehearsing the new persona, your client will need to grasp that the trauma no longer defines her or him and to consider the journey that has repositioned them at the helm. Your client will need to behold and appreciate the world from the new perspective. Finally, forgiveness—of the self, the offender, and any other individuals implicated in the client's pain—will allow your client to be free of the final grip that the trauma has upon her of him. Through awareness, insight, management, and forgiveness, your client will approximate a return to pre-trauma functioning. Issues up for therapeutic consideration throughout the remainder of the client's life may include intimacy issues, spousal miscommunication, unhealthy sexuality, poor self-concept, lifelong need for intermittent psychotherapy, re-victimization, and/or becoming an offender.

You have probably noticed a lot of changes in yourself since you met your new helper and started doing these activities. Think of how you were when you started and how you are now. You were a seed when you started and you are on your way to becoming a flower; but you aren't there yet. Can you see the differences? List some of them.

_____

_____

_____

_____

Now that you can see the change between how you were then and how you are now, imagine the change between how you are now and how you will be in the future. Judging by the differences you already see today, what kind of differences do you see in the future? If you were a seed when you started, what kind of flower do you see yourself growing into? Where are you headed? What kind of differences do you expect? Include differences you wish to see, as well!

_____

_____

_____

_____

_____

Draw the kind of flower you see yourself becoming. Include a lot of detail!

The Rosebush

Have you ever been in charge of taking care of something? Like a pet or your favorite stuffed animal? Or maybe you have been asked to help take care of someone before? Like a younger sibling or an elderly family member. Caretaking is huge responsibility, and doing it well can give us a lot of pride! Caretaking requires two primary tasks:

- Recognizing the needs of the thing or person you are taking care of, and
- Recognizing the vulnerabilities of the thing or person you are taking care of.

All the other parts of caretaking follow these two primary tasks. Look at the chart below to see how each main caretaking task is attached to other tasks.

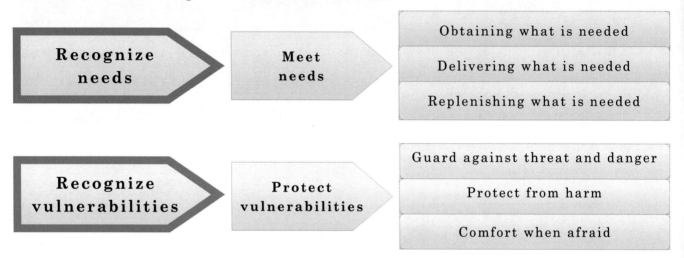

Describe or illustrate a time when you were part of taking care of someone or something. Write in ways that you met needs and protected vulnerabilities.

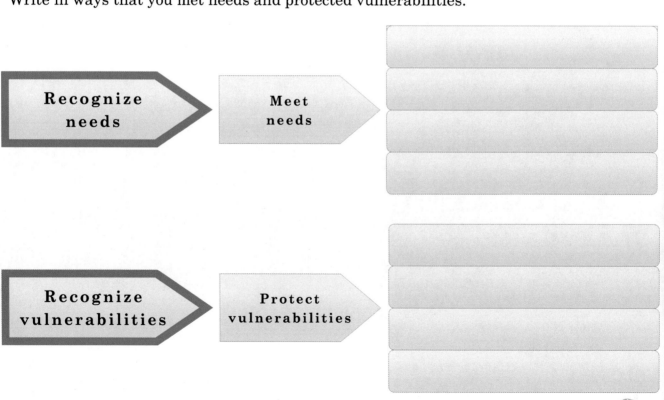

Caretaking is most important when it comes to taking care of ourselves. How can we ever take care of someone or something unless we are first taking care of ourselves? You will be best taken care of when you know how to take care of yourself.

Just like you did in the last activity, try recognizing your needs and vulnerabilities. What are the things you need? Consider everything from your basic needs—like food and shelter—to your higher needs—like love and safety. How do or can you meet these needs? What arc your vulnerabilities? Consider everything from hunger to emotional insecurity. How do you protect your vulnerabilities?

My need for/of [   ] can be met by/through [   ]

My need for/of [   ] can be met by/through [   ]

My need for/of [   ] can be met by/through [   ]

My vulnerability to [   ] can be protected by [   ]

My vulnerability to [   ] can be protected by [   ]

My vulnerability to [   ] can be protected by [   ]

Having responsibility for yourself means more than understanding your needs. It is also about thinking ahead about what you should do and then doing it. It means thinking about what will be expected of you and attempting to meet those expectations. Remember the activities that you did before on finding a way through the woods and on putting problems in their P.L.A.C.E? These activities helped you to develop the ways of thinking that you will need in order to be responsible for yourself. You will need to be responsible for some self-care, your school work, your chores at home, and several other things that your parents, teachers, and caretakers hold you accountable for. When you take responsibility, you have every reason to be proud of yourself!

What are some responsibilities that you have?

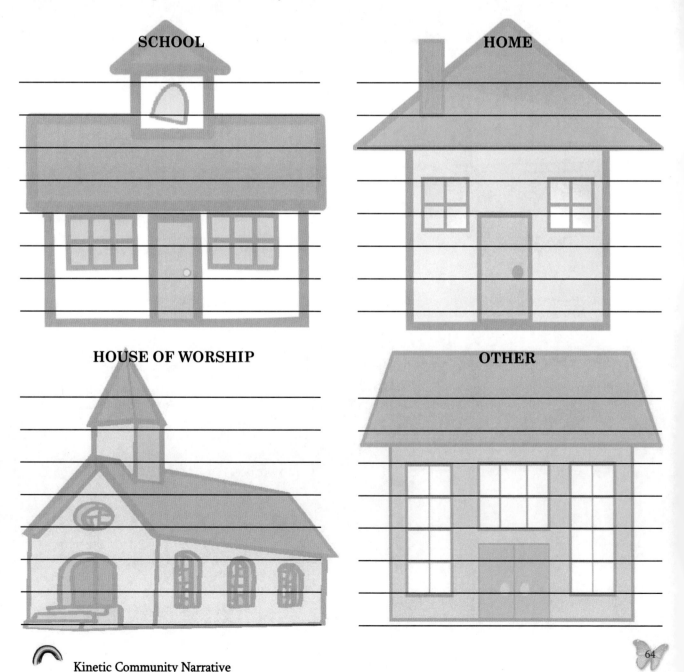

SCHOOL

HOME

HOUSE OF WORSHIP

OTHER

Are you accountable? Ask yourself: Can people count on me to do what I must? Count on me to be responsible? Count on me to do what I say I will do? If so, then you are probably ac-COUNT-able! But being accountable to others is a little different from being accountable to ourselves. Others can see when we are not being accountable to them; so, sometimes, we might only be accountable because we know others are watching. But when we are not accountable to ourselves, we are really the only ones who know. It is harder to be accountable to ourselves because we are the only ones who can make it happen. We have to like and respect ourselves enough to do what is right for ourselves, even when we might not want to or when the task is hard. People who are accountable to themselves are happier because they take care of their needs that only they know about.

Try choosing which of these options is BEST for you, even though it may not be the one you like the most. If you can tell which are the best options, you are on your way to being ac-COUNT-able to yourself and getting even more of your needs met.

Eating sugary candy

Eating an apple or a banana

Holding your temper, even when it's hard

Throwing a tantrum when you are upset

Sleeping late and missing the bus

Waking up on time

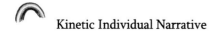

Trusting yourself can be either really difficult or really easy. It depends on how accountable you are to yourself. When we think of trusting ourselves, it is like looking at two pieces of ourselves: the heart that knows what you *want* and the mind that knows what you *need*. If the two pieces do not agree, the mind—the responsible piece—should be the one to make a decision and act on it. Our hearts make the "FEEL-GOOD" decisions, the things that feel like good decisions right now; our minds make the "REAL-GOOD" decisions, the things that are actually best in the long run.

You learned in the last activity that you are able to decide what you need, instead of what you want—how to make a real-good decision instead of a feel-good decision. Think about a normal day in your life—from waking up to going to bed. Think about all the opportunities that you have to make decisions on a normal day. In the 'heart' side of the body below, write at least three feel-good decisions you have the opportunity to make on a normal day. In the 'mind' side, write at least three real-good decisions you would make on a normal day. We are made up of both parts; we just have to let our minds lead the way when the parts disagree. When this becomes the usual, we may trust ourselves more fully!

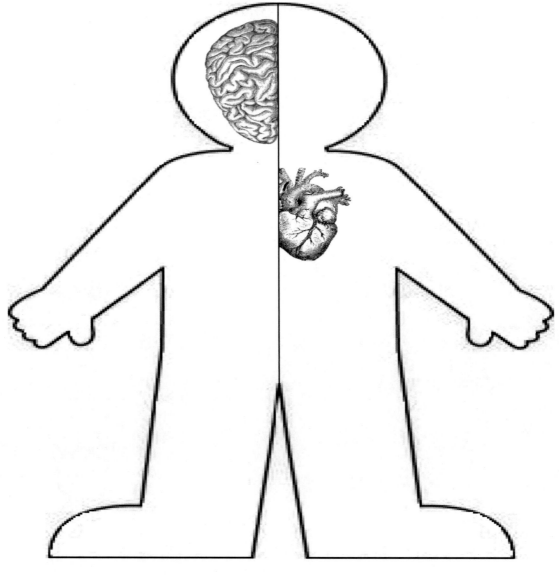

Imagine playing outside on a sunny summer day far away from your house. Imagine how it feels to be outside, what the sky looks like, the sounds you hear. But a storm is coming! How would you be able to tell? What is likely to change about the sunny summer day? What warning signs would you look for? You have seen storms come and go before; you know what to look for. The wind might pick up, you might smell rain in the air, you might notice the sky becoming darker, a siren may sound off. You would have to keep an eye out for these warning signs; otherwise, you might end up caught in a storm without shelter. Knowing and noticing warning signs is a great way to stay safe!

Now imagine that your story—the bad thing that happened to you—is a storm. Like we said, you have survived storms, seen them come and go. What warning signs told you that a storm was coming? That something bad was about to happen to you? Maybe someone started acting differently. Maybe they asked you to keep a secret. Maybe they took you to a place where you were alone. Maybe you got a strange feeling in your stomach. Can you think back to any warning signs?

IV.8 Steer Clear

CAPABLE

Let's think about combining the skills you have learned recently. What can you do when you combine accountability to yourself, trust in yourself, and your ability to notice warning signs? You can avoid more hurt, trauma, and sadness. With your new tools, you can see more clearly than before and keep yourself safe. Making sure that you do not get caught in another storm is a very important part of healing and loving yourself! It all starts with knowing the difference between what you want and what you need.

Can you think of an example of each of the steps below?

When you know the difference between what you want and what you need, **you are accountable to yourself.**

____

____

____

____

When you are accountable, **you make real-good decisions instead of feel-good decisions.**

____

____

____

____

When you make real-good decisions, **you can trust yourself.**

____

____

____

____

When you trust yourself, **you will be able to keep yourself safe when you see warning signs.**

____

____

____

____

Do you know how actors get ready to act in movies and plays? They rehearse! Rehearsal is a kind of practice where somebody practices doing something that they have to do until it is really easy for them. An actor starts out with a script asking them to say and do things they have never said or done before. Then the actor does what the script tells them to do over and over again until they can do it without even thinking. Sometimes, actors have to break the script down into smaller parts and rehearse each part until they can put all the parts together.

The kind of rehearsal that can help you the most right now is practicing what you will say or do in response to warning signs or other negative situations. It will include both words *and* actions. Here are some suggestions of responses to certain situations. Have your new helper, a family member, or a close friend help you rehearse these responses. You can even rehearse alone. The important part is going over your prepared responses over and over again you are like an actor who has mastered a script! Feel free to create and rehearse as many responses to situations as you need.

An adult asks you to go somewhere where you shouldn't be alone with them. They don't want you to tell anyone.		"It isn't ok for me to be somewhere without someone knowing about it. I will have to ask permission first."
An adult says that if you tell their secret, they will hurt you or your family.		If you feel in danger, go outside of your home (school, neighbors, doctor, church) and find someone who will listen to your fears.
An adult says that, if you tell their secret, your family and friends will look at you differently.		Attempt to tell an adult who can help. If you cannot at the time, try telling others until you get help.
An adult tells you, "I'm the adult and you are supposed to respect me and do what I tell you to do."		"Before I can do what you want me to do, I have to tell someone who loves me and see if it is ok."
An older kid tells you that if you don't do what they want you to do, then you aren't cool.		"I don't need to be cool if it means doing things that hurt me or make me uncomfortable."

♪♪ Puppet Interview

Trauma can leave us in a kind of prison. It can make us behave in certain ways and constrain our freedom—make us behave in certain ways we would not otherwise behave. All the things you have learned throughout these activities have helped you to gain freedom from the sadness, anger, and fear that have been following you around since your trauma. With the skills you have been learning, you can keep yourself free to think and act as you normally would without false beliefs and anxieties.

However, with freedom comes responsibility. They are two sides of the same coin! You have the tools now to be free from your trauma. It is your responsibility to use those tools to keep yourself free and really enjoy the hard work you have done for the rest of your life. Use your responsibility to yourself to remain free!

If you are free to

| choose your actions |

Then you are responsible for

| making them safe actions |

If you are free to

| make your own decisions |

Then you are responsible for

| making real-good decisions |

If you are free to

| think for yourself |

Then you are responsible for

| thinking carefully and clearly |

If you are free to

| decide who gets close to you |

Then you are responsible for

| making sure you feel safe beforehand |

If you are free to

| experience your emotions |

Then you are responsible for

| not letting them control your actions |

Can you pair any more freedoms and responsibilities? Feel free to make a whole list!

If you are free to

Then you are responsible for

If you are free to

Then you are responsible for

Think of the last time you apologized for something that you were really sorry for. You probably wanted forgiveness so that you could feel better for whatever it was that you did wrong. While forgiveness can certainly make us feel better when we *RECEIVE* it, it is actually better to *GIVE* it. Forgiveness is a gift that you give to yourself! It is called a gift because nobody deserves forgiveness. It can't be earned, demanded, or paid—only given freely once someone decides to give it. When someone hurts us and we don't forgive them, they have a little bit of power over us. The scar they put on us continues to hurt until we forgive them. We think about how they hurt us; the pain controls our actions and decisions; and sometimes we can even become angry and begin to lose our happiness. When we forgive, we take back the power that person has. We don't even have to tell the person that we forgive them. If you'll never see the person who hurt you again, you can still forgive them in your heart. That way, the pain and the scars no longer control you.

Imagine putting forgiveness in the gift box below, forgiveness for all the wrong things done to you by someone. Color and decorate it any way you like, but be sure to put *YOUR* name on the tag. This is because forgiveness is a gift that you give to yourself!

Shoebox

Do you remember when you first started these activities? You spent some time just learning about new words and other things that you didn't understand because learning and understanding new things gives us more power over ourselves and our lives. This activity is kind of like that, except you will be learning about sex. If you haven't heard of this word before, it is a word describing what two adults do when they share certain special feelings for one another. Try to answer the questions below with your new helper or a trusted adult. For the questions you don't get right the first time, find the right answers by looking them up or talking to a trusted adult about them; then discuss the answers until you are sure you understand. After this, these concepts won't be as confusing or scary to you anymore. You will have the power of knowledge to help you build a healthy future!

1. Do you know any names for private body parts?

2. Do you know what a girl's private parts are called?

3. Do you know what a boy's private parts are called?

4. Whom can you talk to about things like this?

5. What kind of special feelings do you think adults have for one another when they have sex?

6. Do you know any other names for sex? Are there different kinds of sex?

7. What do you think the differences might be between healthy sex and unhealthy sex?

8. Do you know what consent means?

9. What role does the law play in healthy sexuality?

10. Do you think that wanting to have sex is normal or unhealthy?

11. Do you know what the purposes of sex are?

12. Do you know what some consequences of sex are?

13. How do you know when you are ready to have sex?

14. Who can have sex with whom? Under what circumstances is it okay to have sex?

15. Why would someone have sex with a person it is not okay to have sex with?

16. Do you know what masturbation is? Under what circumstances is it okay to masturbate?

17. What should you do if you have a sexual problem?

18. What role do you think privacy preserves in healthy sexuality?

19. What role do you think belief systems plays in healthy sexuality?

20. What role do you think that television, the Internet, movies, and commercials play in healthy sexuality?

 Why We "Do It"

Clinician's Key To Activity IV.12

Below are some suggested answers to the questions posed to the client in Activity IV.12 on the previous page. If you are knowledgeable about the correct and/or suggested answers to these questions, feel free and encouraged to discuss them openly and directly with the client. Be prepared to challenge client resistance or feelings of awkwardness. This is not an exhaustive or definitive list of correct or appropriate responses to the questions in Activity IV.12; they are, rather, suggested avenues for clinical exploration. This list represents an attempt to provide the client with a basic understanding of the scientific concepts of sex, sexuality, and anatomy; the central roles of consent, privacy, and appropriateness; and the peripheral roles of the law, the media, and belief systems. As always, take care to exercise clinical judgment in the avenues you choose to present and the thoroughness with which you answer them. Consider factors such as the client's age, developmental level, degree of trauma processing (how the client has processed similar ideas previously in the treatment process), as well as any other special considerations particular to this client or to the therapeutic relationship. Feel free and encouraged to explore beyond the suggested limitations of this activity as appropriate to the client's particular situation, treatment needs, and degree of curiosity.

1. *Genitals or genitalia, reproductive system, anus, nipples* (as applicable);
   Address any slang encountered.

2. *Vagina, clitoris, breasts;*
   Address any slang encountered.

3. *Penis, testicles, erection, semen or ejaculate;*
   Address any slang encountered.

4. Doctors, counselors, officers of the law, other appropriate professionals, parents or guardians;
   Define and discuss *trusted adult.*

5. Define and discuss *love, commitment, respect, trust;*
   Emphasize maturity required.

6. *Lovemaking or intercourse;*
   Address any slang encountered;
   Define and discuss *oral sex, anal sex, mutual masturbation, fetish,*
      heterosexuality/homosexuality/bisexuality (as applicable).

7. Define and discuss *maturity, consent, pleasure, acceptance of sex as a natural desire.*

8. Define and discuss *autonomy, choice, compliance or acquiescence, coercion,*
      manipulation, age of consent, competence or soundness of mind;
   Emphasize some understanding of consequences required;
   Consider *consent versus assent.*

9. The law defines what is and is not okay to do concerning sex in our society by providing for rights and prohibitions;

   Define and discuss **rape and statutory rape, molestation, age of consent, sex crimes.**

10. Discuss **sex as a natural desire, sexual response and desire as healthy, and involuntary inclinations**.

11. Define and discuss **procreation, recreation (stress relief/ orgasm), pair bonding.**

12. Define and discuss **pregnancy, STIs, sex crimes, emotional damage (to self and others)**.

13. Define and discuss **puberty, physical maturity, emotional maturity, acceptance of risks**.

14. People who have reached the age of consent and are of sound mind may legally have sex with other people who have reached the age of consent and are of sound mind, if they both give consent;

    Define and discuss **privacy, security and comfortability, public indecency, inadequacy of presumption or assumption of consent.**

15. Define and discuss **mental illness, predatoriness and sex crimes, power dynamics.**

16. Define and discuss **masturbation, masturbation as normal, variation in acceptability, appropriate confines, healthy vs. unhealthy frequency and practice.**

17. When you have a sexual problem, you can go to your parents, a medical professional, a school counselor or administrator, or a trusted adult;

    Define and discuss **physiological and emotional issues, curiosity as natural.**

18. Privacy preserves sex as an intimate and valuable dimension in a relationship, privileging only the two participating partners to the shared experience, knowledge thereof, and the benefits sex brings to their relationship.

19. Most belief systems differ on their views of sex and sexuality—condoning and condemning certain practices, partner arrangements, conditions of permissibility, etc.;

    Define and discuss the **right to belief and practice of faith, spiritual conflict** (as applicable).

20. The media harness our natural desire for sex and intimacy to advertise products, to increase the entertainment value of some productions, and to manipulate our thoughts about certain people, places, and things. The media rarely portrays sex for its core purposes. The media presents a skewed perception of sex and can lead to unfair (and unmet) expectations.

    Define and discuss **pornography (unrealism and violence), egotism.**

Think about the last time you went on a trip. Before you left, you probably had to pack a suitcase with everything you would need—some clothes, a toothbrush, maybe even your favorite toy. It is important to think wisely about what to pack so you can be prepared on your travels. The same is true for you as you prepare to finish this workbook. Now that you have learned how to care for yourself in times of trauma, it is time to pack your suitcase with the most important tools you have learned. You will carry these tools and accomplishments with you for the rest of your life! Write or draw the most important things you've learned in your suitcase below.

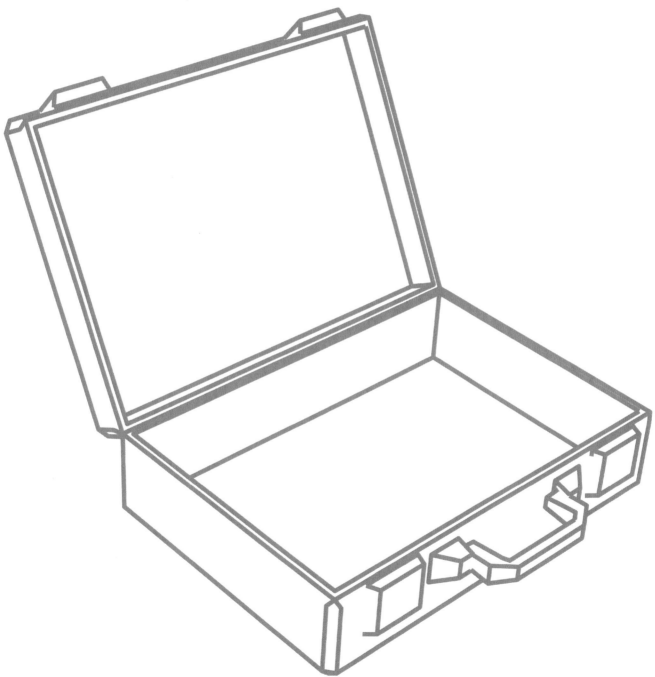

You did it! You have worked hard to learn many new words and new skills, and now it is time to celebrate everything that you have accomplished.

Draw a picture of you and all of your helpers celebrating your success with a parade! Be sure to include any friends, teachers, or trusted adults that supported you along the way. As you work on your drawing, think about including signs or floats in your parade. What do they say? Where is your parade going?

Even though there is so much to celebrate today, sometimes celebrations can be sad or stressful too—it means you have finished one stage of life and are entering another. What feelings do you have about completing this workbook? What was your favorite part? What part was the most difficult? How were you able to get through it?

_____

_____

_____

_____

 Kinetic Support Drawing

Client Certificates

CONGRATULATIONS!

THIS IS TO CERTIFY THAT

COUNTS, is CONNECTED, has COURAGE, and is CAPABLE

AND HAS SUCCESSFULLY COMPLETED A WORKBOOK FOR

THROUGH THE USE OF

EXPRESSIVE ARTS, KINESTHETIC & MUSIC, AND NARRATIVE THERAPIES

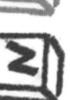

AUTHORED BY BRIGHTER TOMORROWS CONSULTING, LLC

WITH _____

AS OF TODAY'S DATE, _____

CONGRATULATIONS!

THIS IS TO CERTIFY THAT

COUNTS, is CONNECTED, has COURAGE, and is CAPABLE

AND HAS SUCCESSFULLY COMPLETED THE WORKBOOK

AUTHORED BY BRIGHTER TOMORROWS CONSULTING, LLC

WITH _____

AS OF TODAY'S DATE, _____

Bibliography

Bibliography

Adler, A. (2014). *The Practice and Theory of Individual Psychology.* New York, NY: Routledge.

American Psychiatric Association. (2013). *Diagnostic and Statistical Manual of Mental Disorders* (5th ed.). Arlington, VA: American Psychiatric Publishing.

Bratton, S., & Ray, D. (2000). What the research shows about play therapy. *International Journal of Play Therapy, 9:1,* 47-88.

Burns, R. C., & Kaufman, S. H. (1970). *Kinetic Family Drawings (K-F-D): An Introduction to Understanding Children Through Kinetic Drawings.* Oxford, England: Brunner/Mazel.

Dillman-Taylor, D. L., Ray, D. C., & Henson, R. K. (2015). Development and factor structure of the Adlerian personality priority assessment. *Archives of Assessment Psychology, 5:1,* 23-36.

Johnston, S. S. M. (1997). The use of art and play therapy with victims of sexual abuse: a review of the literature. *Family Therapy: The Journal of the California Graduate School of Family Psychology, 24:2,* 101-113.

Kottman, T. (1999). Integrating the crucial c's into Adlerian play therapy. *The Journal of Individual Psychology, 55:3,* 288-297.

Kottman, T. (2011). *Play Therapy: Basics & Beyond* (2nd ed.). Alexandria, VA: American Counseling Association.

Kottman, T., & Warlick, J. (1997). Adlerian play therapy: practical considerations. In J. Carlson & S. Slavik (Eds.), *Techniques in Adlerian Psychology* (pp. 323-337). Washington, D.C.: Taylor & Francis.

Landreth, G. L. (2002). *Play Therapy: The Art of The Relationship* (2nd ed.). New York: Brunner-Routledge.

Meany-Walen, K. K., Bratton, S. C., & Kottman, T. (2014). Effects of Adlerian Play Therapy on reducing students' disruptive behaviors. *Journal of Counseling & Development, 92,* 47–56.

Morrison, M. O. (2009). Adlerian Play Therapy with a traumatized boy. *Journal of Individual Psychology, 65:1,* 57-68.

Norton, B., Ferriegel, M., & Norton, C. (2011). Somatic expressions of trauma in experiential play therapy. *International Journal of Play Therapy, 20:3,* 138-152.

Bibliography

Norton, C., & Norton, B. (2006). Experiential play therapy. In C. E. Schaefer & H. G. Kaduson (Eds.), *Contemporary Play Therapy: Theory, Research, and Practice* (pp. 28-54). New York: The Guilford Press.

Ray, D., Bratton, S., Rhine, T., & Jones, L. (2001). The effectiveness of play therapy: Responding to the critics. *International Journal of Play Therapy, 10:1,* 85-108.

Rogers, C. R. (1951). *Client-centered Therapy: Its Current Practice, Implications, and Theory.* Oxford, England: Houghton Mifflin.

Saunders, B. E., Berliner, L., & Hanson, R. F. (Eds.). (2003). *Child physical and sexual abuse: Guidelines for treatment (Final report).* Charleston, SC: National Crime Victims Research and Treatment Center.

Soole, R., Kõlves, K., & De Leo, D. (2015). Suicide in children: a systematic review. *Journal of the International Academy for Suicide Research, 19:3,* 285-304.

Stith, S. M., Miller, M. S., Boyle, J., Swinton, J., Ratcliffe, G., & McCollum, E. (2012). Making a difference in making miracles: Common roadblocks to miracle question effectiveness. *Journal of Marital and Family Therapy, 38:2,* 380-393.

Sutherland, J. A. (1995). The Johari Window: a strategy for teaching therapeutic confrontation. *Nurse Educator, 12:3,* 22-24.

van der Kolk, B. A., McFarlane, A. C., & Weisaeth, L. (Eds.). (1996). *Traumatic Stress: The Effects of Overwhelming Experience on Mind, Body, and Society.* New York, NY: Guilford Press.

Index of Play Prescriptions

Index of Play Prescriptions

Therapeutic Stage I

1. Kinetic Individual Drawing
2. Kinetic Family Drawing
3. Kinetic Community Drawing
4. Worst Day Ever
5. Knowledge Is Power
6. Normalizing Traumatic Response
7. The Miracle Question
8. As Sweet As Honey
9. Gaining Ground

Therapeutic Stage III

1. Anger Thermometer
2. Five Senses Poem: Anger
3. Anger Umbrella
4. Bill of Behavioral Rights
5. Big Door In, Small Door Out
6. Bubble Breaths
7. Space Invaders
8. How Does The Closet Feel?
9. Safe Keeping
10. Feeling Faces
11. Directed Miniature Play
12. Kinetic Body Narrative
13. First Aid
14. Event Dynamics Map
15. The Three Little Parts
16. X-Ray
17. Roots & Fruits
18. Eggshells
19. Person Picking An Apple From A Tree

Therapeutic Stage II

1. Your Very Own Personality Puppet
2. Empty Box
3. Emotions Chart
4. Bump In The Night
5. Parts Party
6. Johari Window
7. 25 Things I Like About Me

Therapeutic Stage IV

1. The Rosebush
2. Caretaking Project
3. Self-Caretaking Project
4. Kinetic Community Narrative
5. Kinetic Individual Narrative
6. Decision Hopscotch
7. Learning From Experience
8. My Own Safety & Crisis Plan
9. Puppet Interview
10. Balancing Act
11. Shoebox
12. Kinetic Skills Drawing
13. Kinetic Support Drawing

About Brighter Tomorrows Consulting, LLC

Brighter Tomorrows Consulting
Together Tomorrow will be Brighter

Brighter Tomorrows Consulting is a private outpatient mental and behavioral health practice in Griffin, Georgia. We provide clinical services to individuals, couples, families, children, adolescents, and adults as a mental and behavioral health practice within the community system. As therapists, our goal is to help clients uncover their true potential. While we cannot change difficult situations of the past, we can work together to better understand and resolve challenges in the present and future. By applying integrative, individualized therapeutic approaches designed for individuals, couples, and families, we can work collaboratively toward healing and wholeness. Our Core Values include client welfare, professional development, social advocacy, beneficence, non-maleficence, autonomy, justice, and fidelity. The focus of Brighter Tomorrows Consulting is to build toward strengths, wholeness, healing, and self-efficacy.

Incorruptible Seed Ministries, a 501(c)3 non-profit entity established in May 2010, is the non-profit arm of Brighter Tomorrows Consulting. Our organization seeks to improve the mental and behavioral health climate within our community, raise awareness of the importance of mental and behavioral health services, reduce the stigma surrounding these services, and provide no-cost services to those in need who may otherwise be rejected due to their inability to pay. Our organizational goals are to collaborate with community-based programs and initiatives, such as Project Aware, through the Spalding County School System, and the Healthy Children Initiative, with the Spalding County Collaborative, to assist in the effort to close the gap surrounding the mental and behavioral health needs among children, youth, and their families. We have never turned anyone away for inability to pay for services and typically provide over $100,000 annually of charitable in-kind services for the community at large.

About the Author

About the Author

Shannon Eller, LPC, LMFT
CEO of Brighter Tomorrows Consulting

Shannon earned a Bachelor of Science degree from Georgia State University in 1986, specializing in Middle Childhood Education with Teacher Support Specialist Certification. She holds a T-5 State of Georgia Teaching Certificate, and taught for eighteen years prior to earning a Master of Science Degree in Community Counseling from Columbus State University, *summa cum laude*, in 2006. Shannon is dually licensed as both a Licensed Professional Counselor (LPC) and a Licensed Marriage and Family Therapist (LMFT). She is also certified as a National Certified Counselor (NCC) and holds a variety of state certifications including: Clinical Certified Alcohol and Drug Addictions Counselor (CCADC); Co-Occurring Disorders Professional Diplomate (CCDP-D); Registered Play Therapist Supervisor (RPT-S); AAMFT– Approved Supervisor, Certified Professional Counselor Supervisor (CPCS); and Certified Clinical Supervisor (CCS).